Our World of Information

# What's next?

## Instructions and Directions

Claire Throp

KU-213-149

Heinemann
LIBRARY

## www.heinemannlibrary.co.uk
Visit our website to find out more information about Heinemann Library books.

## To order:
☎ Phone +44 (0) 1865 888066
📄 Fax +44 (0) 1865 314091
🖥 Visit www.heinemannlibrary.co.uk

Heinemann Library is an imprint of Capstone Global Library Limited, a company incorporated in England and Wales having its registered office at 7 Pilgrim Street, London, EC4V 6LB - Registered company number: 6695582

"Heinemann" is a registered trademark of Pearson Education Limited, under licence to Capstone Global Library Limited

Text © Capstone Global Library Limited 2010
First published in hardback in 2010

Edited by Charlotte Guillain and Catherine Veitch
Designed by Richard Parker
Original illustrations © Capstone Global Library
Illustrated by Darren Lingard
Picture research by Ruth Blair
Originated by Heinemann Library
Printed in China by South China Printing Company Ltd.

ISBN 978 0 431163 16 1 (hardback)
14 13 12 11 10
10 9 8 7 6 5 4 3 2 1

**British Library Cataloguing in Publication Data**

Throp, Claire.
What's next? : instructions and directions. -- (Our world of information)
025.5'24-dc22
A full catalogue record for this book is available from the British Library.

**Acknowledgements**

We would like to thank the following for permission to reproduce photographs: Alamy pp. **17** (© fStop), **22** (© Stock4B GmbH), **23** (© Jupiterimages/Pixland); © Capstone Publishers pp. **6, 7 & 11** (Karon Dubke); Corbis pp. **19** (Thinkstock), **24** (Ronnie Kaufman), **25** (Randy Faris); Getty Images pp. **5** (Lukas Creter), **9** (Vincenzo Lombardo), **10** (Ableimages), **15** (Thomas Barwick), **20** (Stockbyte), **21** (Yellow Dog Productions), **26** (Paul Quayle), **27** (Steve Satushek); iStockphoto pp. **16, 28** (© Julie Masson Deshaies); Photoshot p. **8**; Shutterstock p. **13** (© Alexander Shalamov).

Cover photograph of boys looking at a map and a compass reproduced with permission of Corbis (Fancy/Veer).

Every effort has been made to contact copyright holders of material reproduced in this book. Any omissions will be rectified in subsequent printings if notice is given to the publishers.

All the Internet addresses (URLs) given in this book were valid at the time of going to press. However, due to the dynamic nature of the Internet, some addresses may have changed, or sites may have changed or ceased to exist since publication. While the author and publisher regret any inconvenience this may cause readers, no responsibility for any such changes can be accepted by either the author or the publisher.

# Contents

Any words appearing in the text in bold, **like this**, are explained in the glossary.

# What are instructions?

People are surrounded by information. Information is what people know about things. Information that tells you how to do things is called instructions or directions.

 A **map** shows you how to get somewhere.

You will often need to find certain types of information. You might need help on how to work a machine or need directions to a particular place. This book will help you find what you need. This book is a set of instructions on finding information.

Reading the instruction booklet can help you to set up a machine.

# Why do you need instructions?

No one person knows everything. This means that people have to learn how to do things. They learn by following instructions.

 Some toys do not need instructions. It does not matter how you put them together.

Instructions tell you how to make things happen. They help because they save you time. If you always had to work things out without instructions, everything would take a very long time.

 Toys sometimes come with instructions.

# Where do you find instructions?

You can find instructions in many different places. Instructions that help you work a machine can be found on packaging or in information booklets.

Instructions that tell you how to cook food properly can be found in recipe books or on food packaging.

On the label:

RN #98832 | CA #34769
100%
Cotone
Cotton
Coton
Baumwolle
Algodon

Washing labels on clothes tell us how to look after them.

People need instructions to help them work out what temperature to wash clothes. The labels in clothes tell us how to wash them properly.

9

# What types of instructions are there?

There are many different types of instructions. When you play football, your teacher or coach will give you instructions on how to play the game. Your teacher may tell you not to run in the corridor at school. This type of instruction is for your safety.

Sometimes you need to listen to instructions.

 Instructions tell you the rules of a game.

Other instructions are written down. You have to read them to know what to do. For example, to work out how to play a new computer game, you have to read the instructions that come with it. These instructions may be in a booklet or on the screen itself.

# Lists

Instructions have to be clear and easy to understand. Instructions are often written as a list using numbers or **bullet points**.

**1** Preheat the oven to 200 °C/ 400 °F/gas mark 6. Put the muffin paper cases into the muffin tin.

**2** Put the flour and baking powder into the mixing bowl. Add the butter. Use your fingertips to rub the butter and dry ingredients together until the mixture looks like fine breadcrumbs.

**3** Stir in the sugar, blueberries, and grated lemon rind.

**4** Use a fork to mix the eggs and milk together in a jug. Pour this mixture into the mixing bowl and stir with a wooden spoon until well mixed. (It will still look a bit lumpy.)

**5** Use the tablespoon to spoon the mixture into the paper cases. Fill each paper case almost to the top.

**6** Bake the muffins in the oven for about 20–25 minutes until they have risen and turned golden. Leave the muffins to cool for a few minutes in the tray. Carefully lift them out and place them on a wire rack to cool them for a little longer before serving.

 Blueberry muffins are easy to make if you follow the instructions.

Numbered lists are very helpful because they tell you in what order to do things. An example of this is a recipe. Instructions have to be in the right order or the recipe will not work. Imagine what would happen if you tried icing cakes before you put the cake mixture in the oven.

 Sometimes you can be shown how to do things.

# Pictures

Shake to one colour

Half fill cap

Rinse - 30 seconds

Gargle - 30 seconds

WOW! - See results

 Instructions on this mouthwash tell us how to use it.

Sometimes pictures are used instead of text or next to text. The pictures still have to be drawn in the right order so that people know when to do things.

Pictures can be helpful for people who speak different languages. If you travel by plane to another country, it is important to know the aeroplane's safety rules. Safety instructions are shown in drawings to make sure that everyone understands them.

 Safety instructions are also read out and demonstrated by a flight attendant.

# Signs and symbols

The red traffic light tells drivers to stop. What does a green traffic light tell drivers?

People are surrounded by signs and **symbols** every day. A symbol is a picture or word that stands for something. Signs usually give basic instructions in just one or two words. For example, on a shop door you will probably see a sign with the words "Push" or "Pull".

Symbols are designed so everyone can understand them. For example, some signs show a red circle with a diagonal line through it. What do you think this means?

 This sign means that you should not drink the water.

# Where else can you find instructions?

Instructions are found in many places at school. You might see a list of school rules on the wall. You might also be given instructions for homework.

SCHOOL RULES

- Walk slowly around the school.
- Put litter in bins.
- Eat food in the canteen.
- Hang coats on pegs.
- Listen when other people are speaking.

 What instructions does your school have?

A librarian or teacher can help you use an online catalogue.

When you want to find a book or other information **source** in the library, you can use an **online catalogue**. This will give you directions on where to find the book you need. There may be more instructions if you click on "search help" or "questions".

# Rules and laws

Rules are a type of instruction that tell you what you can and cannot do. For example, have you been told not to throw balls indoors? This kind of rule is needed for safety reasons.

If you do something that is against the rules, you will probably be told off.

This man is a judge. He punishes people who break the law.

The rules you learn at home and school help you find out how to act in the world outside. Rules outside the home are called **laws**. People need laws so that everyone can live together. It is important that people all know and follow the same basic laws for safety and fairness.

# Maps and timetables

Directions help you find out how to get where you want to go. Most people use **maps** to find out directions to a place. Maps tell you where things are.

 Maps help you to find your way.

Timetables are very important if you are travelling by train or another type of **public transport**. They help you work out when the next train is coming.

23

# Ask someone!

If you are in a town centre or driving somewhere on holiday and you get lost, you can always ask a police officer or a **traffic warden** for help. People who live in the area can often also give you the right directions to a place.

 You should only ask directions from a stranger if you are with an adult.

Sometimes you might be on holiday in a country where you do not know the language very well. Often you can mention the name of a place to someone and they can point you in the right direction.

# Information in our lives

Instructions are important because they help people live more easily and safely. Instructions can appear as words, answers to questions, **maps**, signs, lists, and in many other ways.

This sign means the area is not safe for swimming.

A sign to show where you must not swim would be useless unless it is clear to everyone what it means. For instructions to be useful, it is important to use words and pictures that everyone understands.

 To play a game of football, everyone needs to know and follow the rules.

# Activities

## Growing sunflowers

Sunflowers can grow up to 3 metres (10 feet) in six months. Use the following instructions to grow your own sunflowers.

1   Plant two or three sunflower seeds in a small plant pot.

2   Place the pot in a bright room and water carefully.

3   When **seedlings** appear, pull out the weaker looking ones and leave the strongest ones.

4   When the seedlings have grown big enough to plant outside, carefully remove them from the pot.

5   Dig a hole in a sunny part of the garden. Add some **compost**.

6   Plant the sunflowers in the hole in your garden. Continue to water the plants well.

7   Watch them grow!

⚠ You will need some sunflower seeds and a pot of soil.

## Writing directions

Hide an object somewhere in your classroom. Then write directions for a friend on how to find the object. Choose a starting point, such as the door of the classroom. Write your directions from there. The directions should be simple, such as "Turn left" or "Walk five steps".

## Using an online catalogue

Use the British Library Integrated Catalogue (see Find out more on page 31) to locate your favourite book title or author. Then do the same search at your local library or in your school library. Make a list of the differences between the catalogues. Which one was easiest for you to use?

# Glossary

**bullet points**  used to show different items in a list. Bullet points look like big dots.

**compost**  decaying natural materials, such as leaves and manure, which are added to soil to help plants grow

**map**  picture of a particular area, such as your town, to show where things are. A map often includes roads, streets, parks, and important buildings.

**online catalogue**  electronic list of all the information sources, such as books, films, and magazines, that can be found in a particular library. The list can be accessed by computer. Some libraries have an online catalogue available on the Internet.

**public transport**  vehicles that can be used by anyone as long as they pay for a ticket. Buses, trains, the tube (underground), and aeroplanes are all forms of public transport.

**seedling**  young plant

**source**  place in which you can find things such as information. A book is a source of information.

**symbol**  word or picture that stands for something else. For example, a triangle made up of three arrows is the sign for recycling.

**terminal**  part of an airport or train station where passengers go to catch their flight or train

**traffic warden**  a person whose job is to check parking and the flow of road traffic in an area

# Find out more

## Books

*A Trip to the Library*, Kate Hayden (Dorling Kindersley, 2004)

*My First Email Guide*, Chris Oxlade (Heinemann Library, 2007)

*My First Internet Guide*, Chris Oxlade (Heinemann Library, 2007)

## Websites

British Library Integrated Catalogue
**http://catalogue.bl.uk**
The website of the British Library, includes an example of an online catalogue.

WorldCat
**www.worldcat.org**
World Cat will give you the name of a library near you that includes your favourite book in its collection.

# Index